Contribute!

Contribute!

Start A Successful, Fulfilling Business While Raising Your Kids

TATIANA AMICO

NEW YORK

LONDON • NASHVILLE • MELBOURNE • VANCOUVER

Contribute!

Start A Successful, Fulfilling Business While Raising Your Kids

Published in New York, New York, by Morgan James Publishing in partnership with Difference Press. Morgan James is a trademark of Morgan James, LLC.
www.MorganJamesPublishing.com

ISBN 9781642795509 paperback
ISBN 9781642795516 eBook
ISBN 9781642795523 audio
Library of Congress Control Number: 2019938261

Cover Design by:
Megan Dillon
megan@creativeninjadesigns.com

Interior Design by:
Melissa Farr
melissa@backporchcreative.com

Author's Photo by:
Christy Lee Riehle

Table of Contents

Introduction

▪▪▪▪▪

Hey, Mama!

We live in a time where we have information, tools, and resources at our fingertips. We can literally do anything. ANYTHING. And we can do it from anywhere – chillin' in our beds, chillin' in the car while the baby sleeps and you're too afraid to wake her so you stay in the car instead, or with your booty in the sand looking at the ocean. Whatever your jam is! How cool is that?

Thank you so much for picking up my book!

So, first – please know that you are amazing, and being a mom is AH-MAZING! It is the hardest job out there, and one that comes with very little recognition.

If you are like me, you want more – more than wiping booties, doing laundry, cleaning, cooking, and stepping on legos (legit one of the most painful things ever). No, this is not all motherhood is. But I'll be straight up with you: For a while, that's all it felt like.

Instead, you want more happiness, more laughs, more freedom, more desires, more love, more possibilities for ourselves and our families.

Maybe you feel there is a hole in your life, one that needs to be filled. It is okay to feel that way and to want more. You are allowed to feel what you feel, you are allowed to dream, you are allowed to have desires for yourself, and you are allowed to change and grow as a WOMAN! You are not alone! Throughout this book, you will learn about other mamas who felt the same.

I'm gonna get real with ya. This is not another boring book on business strategy. I do not have an MBA. In fact, I failed my second semester of college and was told not to even bother applying to business school. So I didn't. I never thought I would build a business. I never thought I would write a book. I was also the girl in English class that would get in trouble for looking at the clock because I couldn't wait to get out of there.

After having my son, I kept thinking about it. *It would be so cool to have a biz, bring in some money, not have to work for anyone else ever again.*" And then I would think:

Who am I to even think I can do this?

How do I even get started?

OMG, this is so overwhelming!

How would I even do this with a baby?

I don't have time!

I don't have money!

What am I even going to do? To sell? Sell? Ewwwwww.

And who will listen to me? Or even think about paying me?

I don't know anyone. How do I market?

Do I need a website?

I need to share *what* on Facebook? No freaking way!

But – and this is a big but – those thoughts of building a business would not go away. I have learned that this kind of stuff happens for a reason, and I' m so glad I listened to myself.

I made a decision when my son was a year old which led me to build a very successful home-based business while being a mama. Since then, I've started a podcast, written this book, and I've been able to take my family on trips, the kinds of trips I would dream of. There are so many opportunities that become available to you when make a decision like this.

The biggest thing I have gained from that decision is *happiness*! I have never felt this way before: true happiness. I learned to see everything differently. I realized the importance of growth. After years of putting on masks and not knowing who I was, the masks came off, and I found myself for the first time since I was a little girl. And what's better is that I now know how to pass along what I've learned to my kids.

* * *

You are a smart, ambitious, resourceful woman, capable of doing anything you set your mind to. Now it's time to decide, get clear on what you want, and take massive action!

So I hope you have a big smile on your face, and perhaps you've had an ugly, yet awesome cry because you've already had some moments of, "Yes, I'm awesome!", "Yes, I need to do this!", and "Wow, I'm so grateful this book has been put in front of my face!". Throughout the rest of this book, you are going to learn about building a business that you want, one that is going to make you want to jump out of bed in the morning with excitement, one that lights you up.

I've learned a lot throughout the many years of building my business. I've learned there are ways of doing it that don't feel so good and that by doing it that way, you will not find true success. I've learned that in order to be truly successful, you must learn to do things in a way that feels good for you, no matter what.

I'm gonna get real with you. I'm gonna be straight up with you on what this takes. I'm gonna help you see that you can make this work and that you need to – for yourself, for your family, and for the people out there that are waiting for you to decide and be the light they need to see.

Your whole life is going to change for the better. You are going to transform. And you'll begin to see the ripple effect on your family and every single person that comes in contact with you!

Are you ready to take those thoughts you've been having that won't go away and do something with them?

Are you ready to discover what makes you come alive? Are you ready to share your gifts with the world?

I got you, Mama! I am so excited to share my story, my journey, my knowledge, and wisdom with you and help you realize that you are capable and deserving of all it is you desire for your life.

Chapter 1

My Story

■■■■■

I was always a dreamer. I loved playing that game where I would say where I would live, what kind of car I would have, what my job would be, and then – I forget exactly how – but there would be a circle around a choice from each category. I would often end up with a Lamborghini (Truth is I had no idea what that car even looked like or that I would have to learn to drive stick, but I knew it was a lot of money, sexy, and fast), a mansion on the beach, and doing some cool job where I made a lot of money.

To be honest, I was never thinking about the babies I would have. I was not that girl. I never pictured myself staying home, raising kids, being a housewife, and doing nothing else. Back then, it was all fun and games. Yet, I know a part of me knew I was meant for so much more.

Being a kid is cool. You laugh at the most random things like seeing someone fall on their butt (I watched my kids peeing their pants laughing as they saw this happen on YouTube); you stop mid-walk to pick up leaves and look at ants and worms; you say what you want to say; you say, "No" a lot; you dance like no one is watching; but most of all, you dream. And you don't have things getting in the way of those dreams like thinking you could never have that or do that or the bazillion other thoughts that surface to shut down the dreaming.

Then others (mean older kids, adults, and society) come in to ruin the party.

So that dreamer turned into a follow the crowd-er. You know – go to school, get good grades, go to college, get in a ton of school loan debt, get a 9-to-5 job that barely pays the school loan, get married, get a house, have kids, and live "happily" ever after.

At some point, I stopped dreaming and began doing all the things I was supposed to do. I lost who I was. I spent years not even knowing. Worse, I spent years pushing "me" down. I spent years pushing my dreams down. I spent years talking really mean to myself. And I spent years coping with that by drinking way too much, smoking, partying, drugs, shopping without the money to shop (hello credit card debt), binging on tv, and fast food, being a toxic, negative person and hanging out with people that enabled it all. Deep down I was escaping reality for years. I now recognize that.

I was in total self-destruction mode from around the age of twelve (maybe earlier) to twenty-five.

My Quarter-Life Crisis

I remember joking on my twenty-fifth birthday, while at Cheesecake Factory, reading a Happy Birthday text from a guy I had met in during a "WTF even happened?" week in Miami Beach, feeling like a total loser, and saying, "I think I'm having a quarter-life crisis."

I knew I was smart. I was meant to do big things, yet I had dropped out of college, was living at home and spending any money I made on alcohol and cigarettes… and on chicken finger subs and French fries with a side of blue cheese.

It was my eighth year working at the Guest Service desk at Target and feeling like I was gonna be stuck there dealing with people wanting to return a shirt they bought months ago, that had clearly been worn a bazillion times and washed, claiming they had never worn it. And to top it off, they did not have a receipt and wanted full price. I still have nightmares about working there and cannot wear khaki ever.

One day a lady comes in who I named "The Devil" because she always made the day much harder (side note: I now know she must have had some stuff going on, and I'm sending her love). No joke, every single time she'd visit, I hid in the back.

For some reason, I came out, and I could feel myself about to flip out, so I ran to my boss and said with tears and snot all over my face, "I can't. I have to go."

It wasn't because of that lady. It was because I was having an "Is this really my life?" moment.

What happens after a breakdown? A breakthrough!

After that, I decided I needed to get my booty back to school. I was ready. I was gonna show what I could do. I wasn't gonna be a loser anymore. I enrolled and was told to pursue communications because those that "won't get into the business school" go into that major. [Insert feelings of not being good enough, or smart enough or capable enough].

I went back to school and double majored in Communication and International Business (not through the biz school) and graduated undergrad with a 3.6 or 3.8. I can't remember. Basically, I proved to myself I could.

After graduation, I was gonna travel the world for some big corporation doing big corporation things. Instead, I ended up as a drive-up teller at a bank. It was an international bank though, so one day I would be sent to Europe. I just knew it.

Nope. Any time I applied for a new position there, I got turned down, so I started looking for other jobs. When I landed a legit international biz once again, I knew that was it. That was when I really began to discover how much the corporate cubicle job was not my jam. That was when the thoughts of having my own business began to resurface. That was when I began pushing them down again.

I had to stick to the plan, to the do-what-I-am-supposed-to-do plan.

My King

After having a bunch of boyfriends and a bunch of heartbreaks, plus a bunch of other random relationships to try and feel good about myself, I met the ONE!

I almost self-sabotaged my way out of it at one point because, "Who am I to deserve him?" Of course, I did not know it at the time. I thought I was just playing hard-to-get. Thankfully, he did not play that game, and did not let me slip away. As he says, "I knew you were special."

When I say my man is the most amazing guy ever, I mean it. A total hottie who wants me to be happy. He's an amazing father too, and he washes dishes and does the laundry. Boom!

Our meeting was not supposed to happen, but the universe, God, source energy, whatever you choose to call it (I will be saying the universe from now on), was like, "Oh no! This is happening. You deserve this guy even if you think you don't."

While at a restaurant, I saw this gorgeous guy sitting with a bunch of friends, and thanks to the gin and tonics, I decided why not and went up to talk to him. And the rest is history. Side note: I no longer need alcohol to give me confidence.

Three years later, we were married. I had the wedding of my dreams. And I got to Europe on my Honeymoon.

Babies

While in Europe… Well, we were in the middle of the ocean somewhere. Our honeymoon was a Mediterranean cruise. We decided to start trying for babies because, I mean, that's what you do, right? You're married now. Next step in this plan is babies.

Over a year later and negative test after negative test, I once again began feeling like a failure. I started wondering if all those years of treating my body terribly had caused me to become infertile. It sucked.

But I decided that I was going to figure it out and I was going to make it happen. This was the catalyst for a massive change in how I took care of my body. I began seeking help. I looked up a naturopath, read books, searched Google endlessly, and I even got on the phone with some lady that did some sort of energy healing thing on me. At that time, I thought that stuff was weird, but I was willing to do anything.

Two months later, I was pregnant!

My Honeymoon Freak Out

While in Madrid on our last night of our honeymoon, sippin' on Sangria, I flipped on my husband. I legit lost it on him on our freaking honeymoon. It had nothing to do with him. I was freaking out about having to go back to a job I hated and now realizing I would be going back to doing all the things society told me I should be doing.

Screaming through the plazas, I actually thought to myself, "I'm not going back".

I did. And I did one of my first really scary things. I quit that job. I totally did it like an a-hole and left a voicemail on my boss's phone, but I did it.

This was it. I could start a business. I had the time. I could do it.

And then the "Oh no" thoughts start coming in like:

- How am I gonna pay off those Prada sunglasses I got in Venice? I still have them, by the way.
- How am I gonna pay my school loans?
- I don't want to put this on my husband?
- What am I even gonna do? Well, I put on an awesome wedding, maybe I can be an event planner? Wait, do I need to go to school for that? F*** it.

So I looked for another job. And I got one, and another after hating that one.

Every day on my drive to work, I would think, "But when I do get pregnant, this is gonna blow. I'm gonna have to find daycare, miss the cute things they will be doing for the 8 plus hours I'll be away from them daily, miss their activities, and basically miss out on their lives."

I would daydream about not having to rush around in the morning to take my kids to daycare and get to work on time or deal with calling into work when they were sick. I would think of our summers and how we would wake up and do whatever we wanted. Go to the park, to the pool, to a fun activity. I knew I did not want to work when I had kids.

Just before Christmas, I found out I was pregnant. The day after Christmas, I got laid off. Thank you, universe!

During my pregnancy, I took all I had been doing for my body to another level. I spent that entire pregnancy learning about all things health. Once again, the thought of a business resurfaced.

I could help people get healthy. Yes! That's what my business would be.

Putting on a Facade

Looking at pictures from my son's first birthday party, all I could see in my face was a look of being completely lost. I didn't know who I was, and the fake smile was very apparent.

Everything looked perfect. The décor was awesome thanks to Pinterest. The cake was amazing. We had a bounce house. I… I'm lying… My mom made my son a refined-sugar-free vegan birthday cake with frosting made from coconut milk and spinach for coloring (No joke; you can find this on my blog).

I was miserable and struggling with the fact that I was because "I should be grateful for all of this and for my life."

I hadn't started the business yet. I was sitting around allowing excuses, fear, mean girl thoughts (thanks to Melissa Ambrossini for naming those thoughts perfectly), doubt, limiting beliefs, and a need to be perfect, get in the way. I allowed this to happen for over a year.

Then something went down to light a fire under my booty to make me feel even worse, to finally do something about it.

The Underwear Story

As women, our underwear (It's underwear, not panties. Please never say panties.) drawer is very significant. Seriously. Go look in yours. Is it filled with old raggedy undies? If so, how does that make you feel?

Well, mine was, and it made me feel super low vibe. Is this what my life has become? Have I completely lost myself as a woman? Instead I wanted be a woman with sexy underwear that gives me all the feels when I put them on!

So, I thought, "I'm gonna go get myself some new underwear. Victoria's Secret, here I come!"

But, oh crap! That meant I needed to ask my husband for money. What. The?! I'm a grown woman having to ask someone else for money to go buy underwear!

I broke down. On the ground. Looking back, I believe that was my moment of surrender.

"Tell me what to do."

This was it. I became open. I became open to opportunity, up to anything that would be thrown in my face to get me out of feeling this way, to get me to actually step up and decide to finally go after that business. And I did.

By the way, I did not go out and buy new underwear that day. I did after I started that business.

Some people keep the first dollar they make. I kept that pair of undies.

I Did the Scary Things

I'll often joke that I've learned more from social media and Google than I did in college. Many times, I feel like this is a legit statement. In fact, I built my multiple six-figure business from all I learned outside of school and from people I met online.

Not too long after I lost it over raggedy underwear, during one of my Google searches looking for what I could possibly do from home to make some money helping people get healthy, I came across an online Health Coaching certification. The company would teach me all I need to know to build a successful health coaching business. Score!

The cost for the certificate was around $3,000. I definitely did not have the money. There I was again, a grown woman, needing to ask someone else for money. This time it was my mom. Yes, I had some feelings coming over me – guilt, shame, fear. I might be wasting her money, but I knew I had to. I knew I had to get over all of that and go for it.

This is what successful people do. They do the scary things. That was just the beginning for me.

In less than two years of making that decision, I was bringing in more than at my last corporate job, and by my third year, I had hit six-figures – all while being at home with my son.

This was not overnight, and it took me:

- Working through a ton of fear – fear of failure, fear of success, fear of the unknown, fear of losing people in my life, fear of growth, fear of the work
- Stepping out of my comfort zone every day
- Becoming extremely resourceful
- Becoming determined
- Working hard. Yep, you have to, and let me tell you, I am so proud to be a hard worker.

- A lot of working on my own personal growth
- Investing in myself and people to help me

There have been ups and downs. There have been times that I've questioned myself. There have been times that I've thought about giving up, but what has kept me going is what we are going to dive into over the next few chapters!

"*Creating my business simply made me a better person and a better mom. It helped me tap into the parts of me that had temporarily gotten lost in the world of motherhood. My business is my passion, my outlet, and my reminder that, yes, I am a mom, but I am also a strong confident woman with a dream. It's pushed me to become the person I want to be not only for my children but for myself.*"

– **Rachael Phillips**, mom of 3,
Owner of AKA Supermom at akasupermom.com

Chapter 2

Starting My Business

■ ■ ■ ■ ■

I was sitting on my couch feeding my two-month-old, feeling like I was losing my mind, Googling and trying to figure out what the I could do to help people and make some money doing it, and I came across an online school/course. I believe it was around $3,500 at the time, and I almost pooped my pants and slipped into victim mode because, "There's no way I can afford this. I guess I can't do anything now. My life sucks."

I couldn't get that course out of my head, and I happened to bring it up to my mom, who said without hesitation, "I'll pay."

Maybe you don't have a parent that will do this, but let me tell you, when you know you need to do something, the support will come to you in some way. When I decided to invest in getting help writing this book and found out the investment was $14,000, I did not freak out, even though I didn't have the money. That's because I knew I'd figure it out, which I did. I also know there is always more money coming my way. This is called having an abundant mindset. There is always more and not only with money. Also, do not make the mistake of telling people who are not 150% supportive of who you are what you want because they may attempt to sway you away from your decision. Instead, own that decision. You made it for a reason.

I told a "friend," who immediately started Googling what I was doing because she "cared about me and wanted to make sure I wasn't making a mistake," and came back saying bad things about the school. I didn't need that in the moment. We never need that.

TATI TIP! **Make decisions based on your intuition. Stop asking others. You know. Trust yourself. Nothing is ever a mistake. Nothing.**

I got on a call with a rep in September 2012, and I remember something she said to me that has stuck with me since that day when I told her I should probably wait until my son was older. She said, "Why would you wait?"

She was right. Again, my fear was taking over, and I had to decide to stop allowing that.

I signed up. I did the work, and again, I found myself paralyzed. I kept doing things to keep me from actually starting, like re-doing my office, or looking for other things to learn. That fear shows up in such sneaky ways.

I finally jumped in. For months, I had been sharing value on Facebook and decided I could take on people to help, but WTF was I actually going to do? The course I had gotten came with outlines and help, but it was so not me, and I hated it. I didn't have the energy and passion around it, and therefore, it was really hard for me to promote and more – actually attract my people.

I saw a few clients, and I did grocery store tours, but I was having to make appointments and leave the house, and that did not support my value of freedom. I began resenting my clients and not giving them my all. I stopped.

A few months later, I decided to join a network marketing company that fit my vibe perfectly. It was a nutrition and fitness company, and I was able to provide their tools while I did what I really wanted to do – that is, support and coach. Because I had the energy and passion around it, my business took off. And I fell in love with one of the biggest aspects of network marketing, helping others build businesses.

I invested $140; that was about the last I had on my credit card, and I built a six-figure business in less than two years. The power of this kind of business is the recurring income once you build a team. Before when I was seeing clients, it was one payment and done (or however many times I would see them).

I have learned a lot with my health and network marketing business. I built it quick and not necessarily in a way that felt good to me. Through all of my experience, I have learned how I do and do not want to build a business. I have learned that there are other things I want to do, and I have learned what to do when things get tough.

What this business has done for me is help me grow. It has opened doors for me, allowed me to do all the things I've wanted to do with my family, allowed me to invest in myself like I never imagined (as I'm typing this, I'm also preparing to attend another Tony Robbins live event – the kind of event that changes you, that helps you step up even more), allowed me to invest more in my business and get in front of more women. I'm so grateful for it!

I'm continuing on with it and helping thousands of women begin their own health and fitness businesses, and now I get to take it further and help other women start the businesses they want. This is what this book is about.

So know that, yes, there are many options for what kind of business to start, and when you choose one, that doesn't mean that's it. You will learn and grow so much, and you will develop new skills and desires along the way. It's so exciting.

* * *

I want to share my experience and what has helped me get to where I have with you, to make the process simpler for you so you know what to do and how to start building a successful business you love.

The first step is to figure out what you want and learn how to have a vision for your business, your life, and your family's life. This is incredibly important in order for you to create a business that's fulfilling for you. It's also going to help you get down to the deep reasons why you are doing this, which will push for you to take action, to move forward, and to keep going.

Next, I'm going to get real with you about the things that come up when you step up in your life in this way. It's all the things that have come up for me and I have seen others deal with. I want to make sure you are prepared so you can bust through the obstacles when they come up. In Chapter 10, I'll help you gain the confidence you'll need to overcome anything that comes up for you or stands in the way of you achieving your dreams. You'll learn how to truly become an empowered, confident mama!

Throughout, you will get really clear on what you want and also learn my best strategies for building a business that will work for you and your family because the point of this is to feel good about what you do and how you do it.

I hope you're excited because this is going to be an amazing journey!

> *"I was a stay at home mom for over 6 years, and there was so many times I felt lost, isolated, lonely, and unfulfilled. I enjoyed being a stay at home and I was very thankful that I got to be a stay at home mom for that time, but at the same time I wanted more. I wanted to make my OWN money. I wanted to be proud of my achievements. I wanted to talk to adults! Starting my business has allowed me to meet more people, feel fulfilled, and shows me that I am more than just a mom and wife. I have found myself, gained confidence, and have realized that I deserve so much more!"*
>
> – **Krystal Jackson**, mom of 4,
> Owner of TrinsonLife

Chapter 3

The Foundation of a Successful Business

■ ■ ■ ■ ■

A few months into my business, I went on my first business trip. It was to Cali, and it was awesome. I remember thinking, "OMG! I'm doing this thing!" Of course, I posted a selfie of me on a plane sharing the great news. My first business trip for my business.

I was headed to an event put on by Chalene Johnson, a mom of two and incredible entrepreneur. My life was never the same after that event. So much happened for me beginning with stepping waaaaaayyyyy out of my comfort zone. I left my son with my husband for the first time, and I had to pump everywhere. I was surrounded by hundreds of people I didn't know but who I felt all knew each other. I swear that's the worst. I felt so out of place because of the stories I was telling myself like, "Everyone here is so successful, and I'm just starting out, so they're not going to want to talk to me;" or "I don't deserve to be here;" or "OMG, I totally did not dress right for this" (Side note: Now you'll usually find me attending these events in workout clothes and a messy bun).

But I knew I needed to be there. I knew I needed to push forward. I knew I needed to get over the mean girl chatter in my head and get the most out of the event. I had a feeling it would help me change my life.

A lot went on during the three days, and I learned a lot, but the most transformative part was when I was asked what I wanted my life to look like and what was my vision.

I had been asked various times before what my goals are or what I wanted, and I would freeze and often never respond or completely disregard the question if it was asked in a book. Seriously.

This event was different though.

I was told to go for it. To go nuts writing in my notebook and not to stop. To think about how I wanted my days to look like. How I wanted to feel. What I was doing and to give specific detail.

For a couple minutes I blanked, and the reason I blanked is because I felt fear and doubt. I began thinking, "What's the point of even doing this if it's not going to happen?" Again, I had to stop myself and go for it. Also, there's something about attending live events and being in a room full of people that want success, and you see them doing the work. It makes you do it too. (This also happens when you have a coach or mentor who is on you to do it as well. This is why I always have one, always.).

All of a sudden, I found myself writing. I couldn't stop, and by a minute in, there were tears streaming down my face. Wow, I needed this so bad. I needed to be honest. I think that was the first time I actually really began to believe in myself!

Motivation Is Not What Is Missing

I see so many women say they are missing motivation and, worse, are waiting to begin taking action. If you are waiting for outside motivation to get you going and keep you going, it's not the answer, girlfriend.

I'm going to help you realize what you need instead. It's the thing that's going to pull you to start and to keep going.

Figuring Out What You Want

"I don't know what I want." I hear this a lot from women, and I have been there too. If you don't know what you want or where you want to go, how will anything change?

You picked up this book for a reason. Maybe you know you are meant to do more with your life. Maybe you are sick of having to depend on others financially and cringe every time you have to ask your partner for money. Maybe you feel like you're stuck in a mediocre life. Maybe you want to show your kids what their mama is capable of. Maybe you have a message inside of you that you need to get out into the world.

The first step to discovering what you want is to get real and clear with where you are. You're going to do this by getting clear on how you're feeling in various areas of your life.

Look at each category and give it a number between 1 and 10 (1 being this blows and 10 being this is awesome). Be honest, girl. No judgment on yourself and no shame. The only way to grow and make things better is to witness it first and then take action. So, don't answer with what you think you should say or what's going to make you feel better. Put the number that best reflects how you feel right now for each area below.

___ PHYSICAL HEALTH

___ MENTAL HEALTH

___ FINANCES

___ SOCIAL LIFE

___ HOBBIES

___ RELATIONSHIP WITH PARTNER

___ RELATIONSHIP(S) WITH KIDS

___ RELATIONSHIP WITH [INSERT OTHERS]

___ CREATIVITY

___ JOY

___ EDUCATION/KNOWLEDGE

___ SPIRITUALITY

Note: The first time I did this, I totally lied as if someone was gonna read it and think, "Wow, her life really sucks!" Actually, it was me saying this to myself, not wanting to face it, because then that meant I had to do something about it.

You did it. Yay! Now you can get to work on the areas you want to improve upon. Building my business has transformed my life, and it will for you too! Just wait!

Have a Vision

"If you are working on something exciting that you really care about, you don't have to be pushed. The vision pulls you."

– Steve Jobs

While at that Chalene Johnson event, I also realized that the reason I was so lost, stuck, overwhelmed, and anxious was because I had no idea where I was going. How could I move forward if I didn't even know what I wanted and how I wanted to feel?

So, guess what you're going to do now? You're going to do some envisioning, mama. You're going to have a vision that makes you want to jump out of bed every morning and do the things! How does that sound?

Get out a piece of paper, a notebook, your phone, your computer, whatever, and go for it. Start writing what an awesome day looks and feels like for you. Remember to get very clear and detailed, let it flow, and do not allow mean girl thoughts get in the way. Get emotional. Get raw. Get excited. Nothing is holding you back. This is the start to you believing in yourself and your capabilities.

You can use all or some of these questions to help you:

- How do you feel when you wake up in the morning? What is the first thing you do? What is your morning ritual and how does that affect your entire day?
- How are you fueling your body? How are you moving your body? Are you full of energy?
- How is your relationship with your partner? Do you kiss in the morning? Say, "I love you."
- How is your relationship with your kids?
- How do you act? How do you react?
- What do you do during the day? Are you helping clients online? Are you stopping in to check on your store, restaurant? Are you meeting friends for lunch?
- Who are your friends? What do they do? How do they act? Are they living the lives they want to live?
- What are you doing with your kids?
- Do you have a cleaning lady?

- How much money are you making? How does this make you feel? What are you able to do because of it? Are you booking a trip for your family (without having to look for the cheapest option)? Are you giving to your favorite charity? Are you putting your kids in activities and/or taking them places?
- What has building this business done for you and your family?
- What has this business done for others?
- Do you feel immense gratitude for your life?

Whew! Good stuff, right? I hope you got goosebumps. Maybe you cried. Keep this somewhere you can read daily if you want. I hung my piece of paper up in my office so I could see it every day.

Guess what happened? Within a few months, I was living that vision (or a version of it).

The Missing Piece

The vision is one part of what you get started and keep going, but having a deep deep deep reason why is what's going to take this all next level.

I love helping my clients get deep on this because it is so powerful. What I have seen (and this was me too) is that many would have a surface-level why. That basically means that your "why" is not deep enough to get you to that place you envisioned. Examples of this include:

"I want to make more money."

"I want to lose weight."

"I want energy."

"I want abs."

"I want to travel."

"I want a house."

"I want a better relationship with my spouse."

"I want to build a business."

I ask them to get deeper, and those that do, and continue working on their vision and why, move forward, and don't given up. Those that don't, go M-I-A. I see this happen over and over and over.

TATI TIP! **When you work with a Coach/Mentor, trust and listen to your coach.**

Why do you want those things? What will this do for you and your life? When you answer the first why, and that why again, and then again, and again.

Again, please make sure to say exactly what pops in your head, not what you think you should say. *Note:* It's very powerful to get with someone else to do this and even better with a Coach.

Also, your WHY may change over time. Here's what I wrote when I first started:

Why did I want to build my business? Because I wanted to bring in money for our family.

Why did I want something for myself and to bring in more money for our family? Because I was sick of having to depend on others for everything and worrying about money.

Why was I sick of having to depend on others and not have financial worry? Because I do not want to completely lose myself and my independence. I don't want to get in fights with my husband about money or always be stressed when the bills come in. I grew up seeing that, and I do not want that for me and my family.

Why do you not want to lose your independence or be stressed when bills come in? Because I've witnessed other women staying in bad relationships due to their dependence on the partner, and I don't want that to ever happen to me or for my husband to feel like he needs to have all the financial stress on him. I do not want to feel stress, and I do not want my family to have stress. I want to contribute financially. I want us to be happy.

Why do you want to feel like you're contributing and be happy? Because I don't want to simply exist. For far too long, I sat back and watched others go after their dreams or live a life I wanted. I want to feel capable! I want to show myself and others what is possible.

Why do I want to show others what is possible? Because I see too many women sitting back, unhappy, unfulfilled, speaking so mean to themselves, settling, staying in bad relationships, not going after their dreams, and full of overwhelm and anxiety, and I want to help them.

Why do I want to help them? Because I know that when there are more women being empowered and stepping up, there will be a massive positive shift in this world that will affect us and more – our kids and future generations.

See how deep I went? And why I move on, even when things get tough? And why I will never give up? My why has a bunch of variables in it. Remember to make yours so it truly fits and empowers you!

Now it's your turn.

As Dean Grazioso says in his book *Millionaire Success Habits*, "When we can uncover our true 'why', our driving purpose in life, and translate that into our actions, we provide the momentum we need to push forward, faster than ever."

I don't want this to be something else you read or listen to and one year from now are still feeling the same. I want this to help fuel you to move forward and live your life to your full potential. I know you have something in you to do more. I know because you are reading this book. Give yourself props for that, and now, make sure to do what is going to help you do that. The past two chapters lay out the foundation. You can't build without a solid foundation. Do this and you are setting yourself up for success and the life you desire and deserve, mama.

So, get to writing and visualizing. Have fun.

"Owning a business is what saved me! It's taught me to feel empowered and gain confidence. I've learned that failure is inevitable and if I'm not failing I'm not growing. I used to quit if I failed... Business had taught me to grow from it. More importantly I've learned that true success comes from inner work and feeling at peace from within."

– Kelly Joseph, mom of 2,
Owner of Healthy Revenge at healthyrevenge.com

Chapter 4

Why You Might Want to Say, "I'm Not Doing This."

▪▪▪▪▪

I'm not going to organic-sugar-cane coat this for you, mama. I'm going to be straight real with you: Building a business is not easy.

I want you to know what to expect. I want you to know what will be coming up for you throughout this journey so that you can be like Wonder Woman and put up that shield to it all. By the way, this is what I do. I picture myself as a superhero who is able to block all this stuff from knocking me down!

There are three main obstacles that will come up for you that I wish I would have known about before I started:

1. People in your life, on social media, etc., who do not get it, get you, or do not agree with you
2. You possess negative and limiting thoughts and expectations
3. Challenges and struggles that will come up

I've noticed something on social media which shows what happens when you decide to step outside of "normal." For example, you post about:

- Graduating from college (and being in a ton of school loan debt…Okay you probably don't add that), and get 2637236246 likes and comments
- The (normal) job you got, and get 1722784974749 likes and comments
- Being engaged, and get 3526354848 likes and comments
- Getting married and get 5262486464891 likes and comments
- Being pregnant, and get 677266164786436 likes and comments
- Having the baby, and get 23262661992694629 likes and comments
- Your decision to start your business and how excited you are… Get 2 likes and a bunch of concerned messages and phone calls worried about you, why you aren't getting a real job or just being a stay at home mom, how hard it's going to be, and blah blah blah blah blah
- Completely transforming your life… Get 1 like and people think you're cray

When you do what is expected, you get praised. When you decide to go against the norm, there can be a lot of concern, criticism, and a lack of support. Do it anyway.

Not Allowing Others to Hold You Back

My uncle got really sick about a week before I made the decision to go all in to write this book. By all in, I mean that I invested a lot of money (that I did not have) to get the help I needed to make this the vision and movement come to fruition. Looking back, subconsciously this was most likely a push I needed. The thought of writing a book had been on my mind for years.

My mother had told me stories of how incredibly smart my uncle was. He had so many incredible ideas. When he told others about them, he was told he was crazy and that it would never work; he would lose money. Blah blah blah blah blah!

Guess what? His idea is now an over billion-dollar industry.

All those people who told him that were people who played life safe. They did the school thing to get the certain job that was attached to someone else's dream, not their own.

Here's the thing though. It's usually not done with malicious intent. It's actually a form of love, of protection. Uncertainty is scary, and our friends and family want to protect us.

Something else that may happen is that when you decide to go for it triggers a feeling of "I'm not good enough. I could never do that" feeling in others, and the way they know to make themselves feel better is to pull you back.

I would hear this a lot from my health and fitness clients, as well as the ladies I was helping build businesses. Things they would be told and asked like:

"You're beautiful as you are."

"Did you join a cult?" I love this one, ha ha ha ha ha.

This one that was told to my girl Kat hurt my heart because of the BS expectations put on mothers: "A good mom and wife puts her kids first."

Crab mentality: "If I can't have it, neither can you." The analogy comes from what happens when crabs are placed in a bucket. When one is attempting it's escape, the others begin pulling him down. When you decide to go after something, others may attempt to kill your self-confidence (on purpose or not), and if you are not aware of what is happening, it just might!

When this happens to you, put up that shield, lady, and block the attacks.

The biggest thing that blew my mind (and what I hear from others as well) when I started my business was the lack of support from people around me that – in my mind – should have been the ones saying, "Yes, girl!" Family that has not once congratulated me on all I have accomplished. To be honest, it sucks. So, what I have to do is know that it has nothing to do with me, to continue on, and to be grateful for the ones that do!

TATI TIP! **Be the woman that gives a "Yes, girl!" to other women!**

You might freak people out, but that's on them, not on you. That's their stuff they need to deal with. You need to keep going. I will be there cheering you on.

The Outside Noise

"You can't have it all."

"You can't have your cake and eat it too."

"Money doesn't grow on trees."

"Must be nice to have…"

"She's just lucky."

"You should be happy and grateful with what you have."

"Save some for others."

"It's just not meant to be."

"Life is hard."

"Your life is over once you have kids."

Have you heard some of these before? Maybe you grew up hearing your parents say it (and now, maybe you do too). Maybe you see posts on social media saying this. Maybe you see it on TV. Maybe you hear it at your daughter's dance school by another mom saying that to her daughter and you really really really want to say something because you don't want that little girl growing up thinking that (It happened to my friend).

I can almost guarantee you are hearing it or seeing it, and it may be seeping into your brain, becoming a subconscious thought, and keeping you from going after more.

This is all noise! These are other people's beliefs that they are allowing to hold them back.

TATI TIP! **Listen up, mama. This is important: Don't allow the limitations others place on themselves to limit you. EVER! You are in charge. You are in control. You must have massive belief in yourself and your capabilities. You show them what's possible! Be the light.**

Haters

A memory of mine popped up on Facebook last week about how people can be so mean for no reason, and that was my biggest fear about sharing on social media. That post was in regard to a comment I got on a picture I posted, where they made fun of my pancakes. "Bahahahaha" is what someone posted. About twenty other people wanted the recipe. Thank goodness I got over that because that is, um, nothing. However, that was when it clicked for me.

TATI TIP! **Not everyone will love your vegan pancakes (a metaphor of course), and that's okay. There are plenty of people that will.**

Being afraid of people who didn't agree with me or called me names or talked bad about me or whatever other drama I was creating in my mind was one of the biggest factors in me playing it small. I was so afraid of haters. I was afraid of people getting upset with me because of what I would say. So, I kept silent. I literally stopped myself from spreading messages I knew others needed to hear. And worse, I was not stepping into my fullest potential.

People out there will not get you. They will not believe in what you do. They'll try to pick you apart. And sometimes I feel like they know my deepest darkest thoughts and they pour salt right into in my wound. I've learned what manipulation truly means.

My haters have taught me a lot. So in a way, I am grateful for them. They are often hurt people who hurt people. Insecurity shows up in many ways, including trying to bring others down, and other people's perceptions of you, are not you.

When you put yourself out there, the haters will come, and they will hit you hard. Do not allow others that don't get it hold you back from getting your message, talent, and inspiration out into the world.

Now, let's get to the toughest roadblock that will come up. That roadblock is you.

Fears That Surface

- Taking time away from my family
- Having to spend money
- Losing money
- Not being good enough
- Failing
- The work involved
- What others will think and say
- Marriage being negatively affected
- My whole world blowing up
- Wasting time
- The unknown
- Putting self out there
- Losing people (friends, family, social media followers)
- Thinking things like: "Why bother?" "Others are doing it and better than I could." "I have no extra energy with kids that don't sleep." "What if it doesn't meet my standards/ expectations?" "I'm not worthy."

I interviewed a bunch of mamas before writing this book, and when I asked why they haven't started, these are some of the things they told me. Sound familiar? Is this some of what you feel? You are not alone.

Any big decision I've made has come with fear, self-doubt, and poop-talking myself. Let's take this book as an example.

I did not do well in English class. I've been told my writing sucks. I've told myself, "You're not a writer, so who do you think you are writing a book?" And I'm petrified that others are going to say it sucks.

I literally have to talk myself out of these thoughts on the daily, and I've gotten much better at it. Yay!

To do this is a skill you will need to learn. A powerful skill.

You're gonna talk poop to yourself. Just like you need to become aware of others talking poop, you need to become aware of yourself.

Your brain is pretty incredible. It knows how to stop you from doing scary things 'cause back in the day our brain needed to keep us super safe from like tigers and stuff. Can't step outside because there just might be a big huge creature with massive teeth ready to eat you. Now it's: "Ahhhh, she's about to level up her life. I have no idea what is going to happen. She might get hurt. I gotta keep her from getting hurt."

Not only that, most of us have been taught to do what everyone else is doing. Why you'll get a bazillion likes and comments on the "normal" things people do like get married, but when you do scary "crazy" things, people are like, "Whoa... What is she thinking?"

We're taught to be safe. As I'm writing this, I hear my kids playing, and my mom saying over and over and over, "Be careful; you're going to get hurt." "Be cautious and don't take risks" gets embedded into our brains.

We watch the news or see all the scary stuff happening, and we are filled with fear. Should we know what's happening? Sure, but wow, it's everywhere. The TV, your social media feeds, the magazines at the checkout line in the grocery store, the conversations with pretty much every single person you come in contact with (that isn't aware of this issue).

We're taught to stay comfy-cozy in Mediocreville. But doing that squashes our dreams, leads to settling and conforming, which leads to desires being shoved down, which leads to unhappiness, anxiety, depression, binging on Doritos and cake, drinking bottles of wine in one sitting, maxing out credit cards on things you don't need (Um… This was all me). What sounds better? Going after a better life, a life where you are doing what you were put on earth to do, a life where you are truly, deep down in your soul, happy?

You will lose people along the way. Yep, you will. You will lose people who are not your people, and it sucks. It really does. You are human with human emotions and needs. One of the biggest is connection, creating space for new awesome people to come into your life and new awesome connections. If I hadn't leveled up, I wouldn't have the people that are in my life now.

Let Go of Expectations

In network marketing businesses, there is a lot of emphasis placed on rank (at least the one I am a part of). And before diving really deep into working on myself, the idea of rank had me feeling like I was either succeeding or failing. I was doing awesome or I sucked.

I allowed that to define me as a coach, leader, business woman, and human. I was relentless in achieving that rank, and because of that, I did not work my business in a way that brought me joy. I didn't even realize it until the day came. I did it!

I remember sitting on my couch thinking, "This is it?" I expected so much more. I got so caught up in the hype, and it hit me hard. So hard that the following year took me through a series of breakdowns which I needed!

TATI TIP! **Everything is a lesson and a chance to grow.**

That helped me realize the importance of digging deep into what I truly wanted, and what success and happiness meant for me.

Desires, dreams, and goals are awesome. Definitely have them and take action to make them happen. But also, remember what it is that is in your heart, and recognize the importance of letting go of the "shoulds." It will all feel so much better that way.

When the Not-So-Great Things Happen

The book that helped me realize just how awesome I am is "You Are A Bad***" by Jen Sincero. I read it in like a day when I was a few months into my business. There was this one part about major challenges coming up once you decide to step up.

I didn't recognize it at first when it was happening to me but when a friend pointed it out one time. It was a time I was going to step up in my biz, then all the things start going wrong, and I wrote to her telling her I was quitting. She said, "Go read that chapter in You Are A Bad***."

And now it's all up in my face when it happens.

When I decided to write this book:

- Before I started, I had to figure out a way to come up with the money to make an investment in my coach and doing this thing. I had to replace a $600 tire on my truck.
- I began having the worst pregnancy symptoms I have ever had in my life! Unlike with my other two, for three straight weeks, I could barely get off the couch.
- Then once I started feeling better, my mom had an accident, and I had to travel to a rehab place every other day, and then move her into my house.

I figured it all out. I did it anyway. Because I made a DECISION and was aware of the, "Yo, Tati, I see you are wanting to do some awesome new stuff, so I'm gonna see how bad you really want this" challenge from the universe.

When you are aware, then you can decide that you are stronger than all of this and, therefore, that the struggle does not have to be real. In Chapter 10, I'm going to help you gain some crazy awesome confidence in how to overcome all of this! Yay!

"No matter how many kids you have or how busy it is, if you are passionate about something or feel pulled to it, go do it. Even if it seems difficult in the moment, because when you look at back at the struggles, the hard things made you into who you are. Go forward with it."

– Gaitrie Devi, mom of 3,
Owner of Devi Bollywood Dance,
devibollywooddance.com

Chapter 5

What Am I Doing?

■■■■■

You have a desire to start a business because you feel it would be really cool to make some money from home while being around for my kids. You may also think it's so cool to be a mom and be a boss. You want to feel fulfilled, proud, and accomplished having your own business and won't have to ask your husband/partner for money anymore.

But then you think, "Yeah, that's all cool, but what am I even gonna do?"

Maybe you have an idea. Maybe you have a thousand ideas. Maybe you don't have a clue. In this chapter, you're gonna figure it out.

Years ago while working my corporate job, sitting at my windowless cubicle, thinking to myself, "I'm deserving and capable of more than this," I would envision myself as a rockstar CEO, rocking a power suit and stilettos. But I had no idea how I was gonna make that happen, so I continued on doing what I was doing, and nothing changed.

While sitting on my couch, with a two-month-old attached to my boob, I would envision myself as a highly successful entrepreneur in my home office killin' it as a mom and a boss. Again, I had no idea how I was gonna make that happen, and so I continued doing what I was doing, and nothing changed.

I see this all the time with moms I chat with and help. They have a big desire to start a business but no clue where to even begin.

Here are some ideas I had:

- A green smoothie bar
- A green smoothie truck
- A vegan restaurant
- A wellness center
- T-shirts

I even went to some local small business meetings and support venues to get help with planning, and I met with others who had ideas to do the same. Nothing happened.

What I did learn is that there was a fire inside of me to take action, but what I didn't learn for a while was that I needed to get super clear on what I really wanted to do and what that looked like for me. When you are clear, you'll figure it all out, make it happen, and wake up in the morning excited to work your business, even when things get hard.

Authenticity Is Powerful

"Can you remember who you were,
before the world told you who you should be?"
– Danielle LaPorte

In order to be successful in business today, specifically online businesses, you gotta know who you are, and you have to be authentic.

By authentic, I mean showing the world the real you. And guess what? It's scary A.F. Fear of what others will think of judgment, of rejection. These are reasons why I was not being authentic for such a long time. To be authentic, you need to be vulnerable. It gives others the opportunity to love and accept you for you. It connects us as human beings, and humans need connection. When you see someone being authentic, it is so attractive.

Pretty much every single time I share on social media, on my podcast, on someone else's podcast, even in this book, the fear comes up. I've wanted to puke sharing some things I have, but I know that it's helping me heal and grow, and that I'm helping you.

Authenticity goes a long way. Gone are the days of facades, being fake, sharing the perfect family photos, and not the craziness behind the scenes. Is this only me? Ha ha ha. Maybe it'll work in the beginning, but people are smart, and can read and more – feel that a mile away.

You being the true you, and you recognizing how amazing you are is so important!

But what if you've spent years putting on the masks and are thinking, "I have no idea who I am?" I'm gonna help you out, but I do need to be honest with you and tell you that this will not happen overnight. This is a process. Trust it.

My biggest desire for you is that you begin to own who you are, you begin to own your thoughts, you begin to speak up for what you believe in, and you stop allowing other people blind you from that. Just because everyone else is doing something or doing things this way or that way doesn't mean you have to. When you do these things, it is so empowering.

The Woman Behind the Mom

Ready to get some clarity on who you are, lady? On who the woman is behind the mom?

To help you accomplish this, I'm going to give you some questions to ask yourself.

Questions are powerful. So often we float through life and don't stop to take a moment with ourselves and ask. You will gain some pretty awesome self-awareness that will help you move forward.

TATI TIP! Stop should'ing on yourself.

What does that mean? When something pops in your mind, go with it. Do not allow the, "but I should feel this way" or "but I should do this," etc., get in the way. Shut that noise down.

Something else that has held me and a lot of the women I've worked with back is comparing. It stills comes up frequently, but I have learned to catch myself, so learn to do that too. Even as I write this, I think of all the awesome books I've read and begin to compare. But they are not me. I am not them. We are all awesome and unique in our own way.

- What did you want to be, do, and have when you were a little girl?
- What is your story? What struggles have you had? What have you overcome?
- What have you learned?
- What are you passionate about?
- What makes you feel alive?
- What can you talk about for hours?
- What are you good at?
- Is there something specific people come and ask you about/ for advice and tips on? Is this something you like to give advice on?
- What are 5 things most people don't know about you?

- What are your core values? (examples: Health, passion, family, fun, freedom, peace, fulfillment, connection, individuality, energy, appreciation, empowerment, gratitude, connected, open-minded, optimistic, wealth, action, abundance…)
- What do you want to be known for?
- What do you want more of in your life?
- What do you want less of in your life?

For me, it took more than simply answering questions like this. It has took experiencing different things, stepping outside of my comfort zone, failure, guidance from others, and assessing my value, and investing in my personal growth (more on this in Chapter 10).

Your Successful Business

"Success is liking yourself, liking what you do, and liking how you do it."
– Maya Angelou

Let's get clear on what you'd love your business to look like. You want one that feels really good to you. When you are building a business you love, you will continue on.

After all those ideas I had for a business (the green smoothie bar, wellness center, etc.), I realized that health is the one thing they all had in common. I wanted to help people be healthy. I also realized that I did not want to be tied down to a brick and mortar, have employees, or have to invest a ton of money to get started.

I saw so many building businesses online helping others, so that is what I decided to do. When I began my health coaching business, I pictured a cool space in my home where clients would come and it'd all be so easy. What ended up happening is I was meeting people at Panera, and I also quickly realized I did not like having to leave my house or see clients in person. That meant I'd actually have to get dressed, ha ha.

Now, if I'm on a call with clients, I'm usually in pj's or workout clothes. Did I mention I like to do things the way I want and when I want? So for me, having an online business was the kind of business I wanted, and I knew would make me feel good.

Here are some questions to answer that will help you gain clarity on what you want for your business:

- What do you want to help people with?
- What do you want to help people overcome? What problem do you want to solve?
- What can you create that will help people with the last question?
- How do you want to feel in your business?
- How do you not want to feel in your business?

- How do you want your business to look? Is there a physical product you want to sell? Are you selling yourself (you know what I mean, ha ha)?
- What do you see yourself WANTING to do in and for your business? Does this include having a brick and mortar? Is it something you'd want all online?
- What does success mean to you?
- What does a successful business look like to you?
- What does success all around in your life look like to you?

By simply answering these questions, you have gained massive clarity.

Please remember, you will continue to learn who you are as you move forward. You owe it to yourself to do this. You deserve it. Please do not stop. Please own who you are. Please share yourself with the world because there is at least one person out there who needs you to do this.

"Because of starting my business, my attitude has changed. I'm not depressed anymore. I have taken control & responsibility for my own dreams & desires."

– **Cathleen Crobons**, mom of 4,
Owner of Healthy Mom on a Mission,
healthymomonamission.com

Chapter 6

Your Ideal Customer

■ ■ ■ ■ ■

Back in 2013 when I started my business, my thought was, "I want to help people get healthy." WTF does that even mean, and who are these people? To no one's surprise, not much happened when I started, and I was having people come to me, or referred to me, who were so not my people.

I was a total newbie and willing to take on anyone. It took me a few years to learn that is not how I want to build my business.

I was scared though. I felt like if I narrowed who I wanted to work with to one specific person, I would miss out on a ton of potential clients. If you feel this way too, please know that *if you are talking to everyone, then you are talking to no one.* About every single business coach I have ever worked with has said this.

To calm that fear for you, I want to remind you that in order to really feel joy in your biz, you want clients/customers who are your people. Also, know that people who don't fit your person exactly will still come to you.

My ideal client is a mom of a certain age, yet I attract tons of women that are not even mothers. My podcast is called Hot Mama Movement, and I have so many listeners who are not mothers and love it. This helped me realize that I could still help other women that were not moms.

Another mistake was I wasn't getting into my ideal client's head. I was putting out what I thought she wanted and needed. One time, I used a picture of a girl frolicking in a field for some marketing (I still laugh about this… Sometimes you have to). My girl didn't want that. She wanted to be able to go to a party without stressing about the number of cookies she would end up eating or not feel horrible looking in her closet because she didn't have anything to wear to the party.

Now it's time to get clear on who your person is and how you're going to solve her problem (i.e. what you'll be offering her).

Also, please know that this clarity is foundational. To have the best results for your biz and to make things much much easier, this must be done before you move forward. It also helps to get guidance on this. For a good three weeks, I felt like I knew who I was writing this book for. One five-minute call with my coach helped me get super clear and has made the whole process so much smoother and happy for me.

Who Is She?

Note: 1. Your ideal person might be a dude, but throughout I will be using "she/her." You switch up yours to your wants; 2. Not all questions will pertain to your biz. You'll know which ones do. Answer those; 3. Your person may be the old you, the you 10 years ago, 5 years ago, 1 year ago, a month ago.

Pull out some paper, your laptop, whatever, and write it out. This is fun. I'm going to be totally honest. For me, this has been that thing I always put off. I did not find it fun. I would get all freaked out about it and then not do anything. If this is you, flip the thoughts in your head to something like, "I'm excited to get to know my person because then I will be able to create exactly what she needs. It will help me have an awesome biz."

Questions to Get to Know Your Person:

- What are their demographics? Age, gender, marital status, income, education, location, job, etc.
- What is she into? Shows, books, blogs, magazines.
- Does she have any hobbies?
- Is she content with their life?
- Does she feel fulfilled?
- Does she spend time and energy in a way they want to?
- How does she want to be different?
- Who does she want to be, and what does she want to have?

- What are her fears?
- What does she worry about?
- What keeps her up at night or wakes her up at night?
- What stresses her out?
- What does she secretly wish was true about her life?
- What is she searching for on Google or Amazon to help her fix her problem?
- What has she tried to solve her problem but has not had results with?
- If she does not get your help/buy your product, how will she solve her problem? Or will her problem even be solved?
- In her words, what is not solving her problem and costing her?
- If she had a magic wand and could change one thing in her life instantly, what would it be in HER words?
- If she solves this problem, how does she think her life will be different?

Make sure to think deep. Perhaps if you sell crochet unicorns, you may feel like, "Who has a problem and the solution is a crochet unicorn."

I had a problem and needed a crochet unicorn, and I bought one for $40. I have a friend who is having a baby who also happens to love unicorns. I also love getting things that you don't find at Target that everyone and their mother will have. I love unique gifts, and I love supporting moms with businesses. I am also willing to spend more money on something hand-made and different. So that is what I did. I am her ideal client.

Additional Help with This:

- Give her a name and write out a narrative about her, like a story.
- Create a physical board (like a vision board). Find a picture of what your ideal person looks like, and add what she would be putting on a vision board. You can also make one on Pinterest or use something like canva.com and add words and pics.
- Interview people who you believe are your person and ask them some of the deeper questions from above. Then use words that they use in your marketing, etc. Make sure you let them know it is a safe space for them to open up.

Once you really get to know her and what she needs, become her bestie. What are you going to provide her? As you found above, your person has a problem that needs to be solved or a desire that needs help to be fulfilled. Think about her problem what she wants and what she needs. When you have this down, you can begin developing what you will be providing, as well as, the information you will put out into the world, which is was will attract your people to you.

You Don't Need to Know It All

Abs! I need abs before I can help anyone get fit. This is what I thought. I fell into: "I have to be perfect, and I need to know it all before I can even start my business." I was so afraid that people would think I was a fraud or didn't know what I was talking about. I was afraid to eat a cookie because then I would be found out!

Then I learned two very important things: 1) I did not need to be perfect, and 2) I'm at least one step ahead of at least one person and that is the person that needs me. If you can help your person solve her problem, then that is enough. You are enough.

The cool thing is that as long as you (which you will need to do) keep working on yourself and learning, you will grow. *Note – as you grow, you'll find that your ideal client may change, and that is okay. Who I work with now is very different than when I started, and I'm adding other aspects to my business, so I actually have a couple different ideal clients.

You Can Say No

So many people think I'm joking when I say I will absolutely not take on male clients, but I'm not joking. I won't. I don't want to. I can say, "No." I can say no to anyone who gives me bad vibes or who I believe is not a good fit for what I have to offer.

In the beginning of my business, I was taking on everyone, and I would find that my soul was getting sucked dry by people who didn't do a thing, were not working on their stuff, and taking it out on me, talking smack about me, and more.

Now I am very clear on my messaging and who I will work with, and I am okay with saying, "No." I'm here to help women who want to change their lives and are willing to do the work.

Building my business has helped me go from a people pleasing enabler to a woman with boundaries that says what she wants and gets it. 🙌

Start Attracting People

I hear things all the time from clients like:

- "I can't get anyone to buy from me."
- "No one is interested."
- "People say they want help, but then they never respond to me."

You want to be attracting your ideal client. When you know your person and you are vocal about how you can solve her problem, she will come to you. I'm talking your soulmate client, the client that begs you take her on as a client and wants to pay you, and the client you love showing up for and/or creating for.

Next, in Chapter 8, I'm going to hook you up with strategies on how to do this and how to build a business in a way that brings you joy.

"I've gone from having extreme anxiety about spending an extra dime, second guessing every decision I would make, and being very negative both about my life, and how I treated my body. Once I started working on building my dream, I turned into a strong woman and mother. My entire outlook on life has changed. I still struggle at times, but I know that with daily effort, will power, believing in myself, and never giving up, that I can have the life that both my children and I deserve to live. The best part about all of it is that my children will grow up believing they can have that too. They'll look back and know that they can be there for their own children while still building a life and a business of their own."

– **Angel Middagh**, mom of 4,
Owner of Fit and Free Company
at fitandfreecompany.com

Chapter 7

Making Your Business Work for You

■ ■ ■ ■ ■

Sitting in my newly decorated office (all the furniture from Ikea), I stared blankly at my computer screen… for weeks! My whole attitude was, "I have no idea what I'm doing, so I'm going to waste time and energy doing things that won't bring in money because really I'm actually afraid to figure it out." This same attitude has also shown up for me in ways like taking a ton of courses, writing unnecessary blog posts, scrolling social media, etc.

The fact is I had all the intentions, but I wasn't doing the work.

Then when I finally started getting over myself and taking intentional action, the whole "OMG this is so hard with a kid, cleaning, cooking, food shopping" attitude started popping up. If you are having this feeling (or something similar), I'm going to give you some ideas and strategies to make your biz work for you and your life!

Ideas for Your Idea

We live in a world now where many have lots and lots of opportunities. So when I hear people complaining about being broke and having no idea what to do, it blows my mind. I also have to take a step back and remind myself that I was there at one point. Here's why I'm different: I stopped complaining, and I made a decision to figure it out, and I continue to every single day.

We also have many options for the kind of business to build, which include creating an online course/teach/coach, affiliate marketing (getting paid by companies to share their products), becoming a virtual assistant, joining a network marketing company, creating a product, and being a freelancer – where you can use your skills in any area: writing, graphic design, accounting, customer service, legal, marketing, translation, and so much more! There are great sites already created for people to find you, such as upwork.com where I hire people from all the time, and I specifically look for moms!

These are some ideas. There are pros and cons to each, and you'll want to make sure and choose something that is aligned with what you want your life and business to look like, along with your values (refer back to Chapter 6). The opportunities out there are endless if you open yourself up to them.

Each of these come with different ways of implementing and finding success of course, but the basic strategies I give will pretty much apply to all.

The Big O

No, I'm not talking about that one. Although, I truly hope you are getting that one consistently. ;)

It's the word you keep telling yourself that makes you feel like you have a ton of bricks on your chest and is keeping you from moving forward: overwhelm.

I'm pretty sure I'd be a millionaire if I was given a dollar every time I heard a woman use this word and, worse, allowed it to keep her from moving forward.

We all have a ton of things going on. We all have crappy things happening to us. Whether we find success or not often depends on how we decide to deal with the chaos we are given.

I get it. I remember thinking of all the things I needed to get done in a day plus all the things I needed to do for my business, and I would freeze. Then months would go by, and nothing happened. I was creating so much drama in my head and freaking out almost every day. I'm not joking. Once I asked my husband, "What is something I say often?" and he told me, "I'm freaking out!" Holy wake-up call! I didn't want to be that person.

Think about what happens when you use words likes stress, overwhelm, anxiety. I know when I hear others say them, I immediately feel stress, overwhelm, and anxiety.

What I learned was that I needed to 1) become aware of what was making me feel that way, 2) change my words and thoughts, 3) take action no matter what (do something to move towards your goal, no matter how small), and 4) ask for and receive help.

I was chatting with one of my clients the other day, and she brought up overwhelm. She said she felt herself slipping into those thoughts but used the work we have done together to pull herself out. She is a mom of two, who works, has a business, and at the time of this conversation, was single mom-ing it and dealing with some family issues. She shared how she recognized what she was thinking and why, and she was able to stop herself from the downward spiral that could have happened. To do this is incredibly powerful, and it will help in all areas of your life, as I have seen it happen for her and so many of my other clients.

You Do Have the Time

Pretty sure I said, "I don't have time" 13778379797940101739 times – maybe more times before I began my business (which kept me from starting it sooner). I have since learned a lot in regards to time, and a lot had to do with working on myself.

Here are some of my biggest tips to create more time!

1. Check your thoughts because this is the most important part. If you believe you don't have the time, then you don't. If you believe you do, then you will.
2. Stop using the word, "busy." What kind of message are you putting out there? And I feel like everyone says this. You ask how they are and the answer is, "busy." Decide instead that you have an awesome life *full* of awesome things going on.
3. Value time. Stop wasting it on things like complaining, thinking you can't, and waiting for something to happen.
4. Value and respect other people's time. If you're always late, work on being on time, and don't flake out on appointments. It's not cool. Am I right? If you must miss something, let the person know, and be honest.
5. Know what you need to do, and chunk the big task into smaller tasks. When I thought about writing this book, I began going back to my old thinking and freaking out, but I knew I could not allow myself to get paralyzed. I had to get this done. So thanks to my coach, I created an outline for it, and added what I would put in each chapter. My brain was immediately happy. I tell the same to my business and health clients, to know the big tasks, and then chunk them down.

6. Take an inventory of how you are spending your time. Like with your health, awareness is going to be a big part of this. What are you spending your time doing? What are your time suckers – social media, tv, laundry, picking up toys, driving everyone around to everything? Eliminate media distractions. Think of how easily it is to get sucked into newsfeeds, email, and TV. I'm not saying not to do those things. I'm saying become aware and schedule time for them.
7. Say, "No!" Take a moment to think if you are constantly putting others before yourself. Think if you are always saying, "Yes" to things that are actually taking time away from the things you need. *You are allowed to put yourself first.*
8. Set boundaries. This is for your life in general with friends and family but also in your business. I've learned to set expectations with my clients and what they can expect from me. Most of what I do is inside Facebook groups or in other ways I have set up, and I won't allow things like text messages or phone calls (unless they have paid me a premium or we have a date and time set up). Set boundaries, and if people don't respect them, learn to get firm. And this is hard. You are not mean for setting

them straight, and some people will try make you feel like you are, but many more will respect you.

9. Get help. When I decided I was done doing everything on my own and began asking for and getting help, everything changed. Ask a family member or friend to spend time with your kids. Tell your husband to step up if you need to. I don't remember the last time I did laundry because my husband stepped up. You can also invest in help. Get a cleaning lady. Get a virtual assistant to do tasks you don't want to do. Also, invest in mentors and coaches to help you. I was so afraid to do this for financial and control issue reasons and had to get over that quick. I have an assistant doing things I hate doing, and I am consistently hiring coaches to help me. This book would not have been written without one. Getting help has been life changing. You will see results a lot faster and get a massive return on your investment
10. Plan your week. What I mean by this is know what you have going on during the week. Are the kids in school? Are there activities they need to go to? Do you have things going on? Then decide when you will focus, and get things done around all of that. It's amazing what you can do with an hour when you know what you'll be doing, are focused, and take action.

Denise Duffield Thomas, mom of three, author, speaker, Money Mindset mentor, and self-made millionaire, in an article titled *I'm A Self-made Millionaire and This Is Exactly How Much Help I Have At Home*, said, "… for some reason, a woman outsourcing home help is secretive and taboo. I'm afraid of being told I'm lazy, out of touch or a bad mother, despite the fact that my husband benefits too!"

TATI TIP! **You can have it all, but you don't have to do it all.**

Take Time Off

You can take time off. Myself and pretty much every single business owner I chat with, has had the belief that, "If I take time off, my business is going to fall apart." You'll see a lot of talk about hustling, and yes, you have to work hard, but please also listen to yourself and take care of you. If you need to Netflix binge on "The Office" for a day or two, do it, as long as you don't allow it to go on for too long. When you go on a trip with your family, take that time to be present with them. It will not all fall apart. It will not all fall apart. Can you tell this is one of my biggest struggles? I'm still working on this.

How to Get Everything You Want

Now that you have decided that you will not allow overwhelm to run your life, and that you do have time (or you will figure out how to), it's time to figure out what you want and how you're gonna get it.

Goals. Goals. Goals. If someone told me I needed goals one more time, I was gonna lose it, ha ha.

I knew I needed to have a target, or I'd be doing random things, but I later learned to do it in a way that felt good to me.

No matter how you word it, you'll need to figure out what you want from your business. How will your business help you contribute?

Before you get started on these questions, you are allowed to dream BIG. You are allowed to change. You can be, do, and have ANYTHING you desire. Let's do this!

Steps to getting anything you want:

1. Choose a timeframe for your goal: 21 days, 30 days, 60 days, 3 months, 6 months, 1 year.
2. What is your goal/outcome? Make sure to be specific.
3. Does this goal excite you? Does it inspire you? Is it compelling?
4. What is the date it happens? What is the time?
5. What resources do you have already and/or what resources do you need to have in order to achieve it? If others have

achieved the goal, what have they done? What do you need to learn? Who will you seek help from? What and who will you invest in to help you get there quicker?

6. Chunk it down. What do you need to do/achieve daily, weekly, and monthly to achieve the goal/outcome? What will be happening to show you are progressing?

   Daily:

   Weekly:

   Monthly:

7. How will you feel when you hit that goal? Close your eyes. See it happening and feel the feelings.

I hosted a workshop with this exercise, and the results for the women that did it, was pretty amazing – myself included!

One of the ladies decided she would pay off debt, saw herself doing it, and she did it.

This is powerful because you are not only setting goals but you are seeing it come true, and you are feeling it as well. One of the most powerful tools to add to your tool belt is to begin believing it is happening and feeling it happening before it actually does. This can take time, so keep doing this exercise with your goals (and not necessarily only for your biz), and it will become easy!

Now It's Time to Start

"You don't have to be great to start.
But you have to start to be great."
– Zig Ziglar

Seriously though – please stop waiting, mama!! It's time to do this thing!

You do not need a certification or fancy degrees or whatever for most things. If you are providing legal advice, then yes, you will probably want to be a lawyer. But I don't want you holding yourself back from being a coach or teaching something because you think you need a certification or a bunch of letters after your name. I have invested thousands on help from mindset and business coaches, and I have not once looked into their credentials. Why I bought from them is something we'll get into in a bit.

Ironically, I did get a certification. Why? Because I thought I needed to. The truth was delaying my start. Often we do this (#Guilty). We go on a learning rampage because we feel all cozy and safe keeping us from actually doing the work!

I'm all for learning, so definitely get all the help and certifications you want, but make sure you aren't allowing it to keep you from moving forward.

Looking back, I am grateful for the experience. I actually joined the online course/certification I did because it also came with learning how to start a business. That is the part I really needed.

You also do not need to wait to have a website, logo, biz name, etc. Just start. Now!

Now that you have strategies and tips to build a successful business that feels good for you, let's get to what I see so many women fear around building a business: selling.

"My business has helped me personally and professionally. As much as I loved being a teacher, I feel so blessed to raise my kids and to harness my schedule the way I need it to be. The work I do is profound and I love helping others and my family as well."

– **Natalie Ryan**, mom of 2,
Family Constilation Facilitator at natalieberthold.com

Chapter 8

Sell in a Way That Feels Good

■■■■■

Any time I would think of selling, I felt like throwing up. That's gross, but I'm serious. All I could think about were annoying salesmen or telemarketers. You know, the ones that are so good at getting you hooked on their questions and then reel you in and you can't say "no."

Here are some things that would come up for me and others I've worked with around selling:

- Fear of the above and being "salesy"
- What would people think?
- How could I charge to help people? Who am I to do that?
- No one will pay me for this.

Here's what I discovered:

- When you sell in a genuine way, it does not feel gross and you will know. Your instincts are powerful.
- I've been able to use the money I've made to invest further into my business and do things like write this book in order to reach and help even more people.

- I get to pay other people, like my assistant, coaches, etc. for their services.
- I can to do all the things for myself and my family.
- I can give.
- I deserve to get paid for what I do – for the energy and time involved.
- I help people get to their desired outcome much faster than if they were trying to do it on their own. Or for many – at all, as they most likely would not do anything without my help.

I have to tell you this: you must believe in yourself and what you offer, and making sure to work on yourself to be your best will be vital in building a successful and fulfilling business (more on this in Chapter 10).

In this chapter, I'm going to help you lose your fear around selling, feel much more comfortable doing it, and help you see why it's important that you do and that you get paid.

Listen

I would often tell my team and my clients, "Don't puke on people." What I mean by that is when someone asks how you can help them, don't go on and on about what you provide or what your product or service will do for them because how do you even know?

Instead, you must learn to ask questions, listen, and understand their wants and needs because it's not about the product or service. It's about their needs, wants, and goals.

Once you have this information, you can become a problem-solver and give them what they want. This is why I had you do the work in Chapter 7. Telling people what they need and want won't do much, but listening and understanding what they truly want and then offering your solution will!

Energy Is Everything

People can sense your energy in what you do and, yes, even through a social media post. You must love what you are offering and selling. You must know that it's that thing that your ideal person is looking for. When you have passion around what you provide, your passion and energy will show, and it's soooooo attractive. It's not pushing. It's attracting. And this is what you want because, in the end, do you really want to be working with or selling to people who don't fully believe in what you provide? I'll answer that for you – nope.

There are few that make me gag that I see a lot especially in network marketing. 1) People are told to send random messages (many were copy and paste, and sometimes I would get one from someone I never talked to or with someone else's name, ha ha… Not a good way to start things off) to everyone and their mother, and 2) using social media posts that "worked" for someone else or that everyone else is doing. Ever notice this?

From the beginning, these two things felt off for me, and I decided to follow what other business coaches were teaching, and that was attraction and authenticity. Sounds much better, right?

Again, it's about energy, passion, and authenticity = attraction (and not feeling gross).

Why Are You Doing This?

What is your ideal customer gaining from buying from you? How will she feel? How will her life change? How will her life be better? When you answer these questions and answer them in a way that gives you chills, you will want to sell. You will want to share what you offer to the world because you know in your soul, that someone needs it, and will be better with it. Yes, even if you're selling a crochet unicorn. I get to have that feeling of seeing my friend with a huge smile and saying, "Oh. My. Goodness! This is amazing!"

If you have a product or service that you know is amazing, that will make people giddy with excitement or will help them get to a place in their life they dream of, then you must sell it like crazy. Own that.

If you still aren't feeling it, then this is an area to work on. Get deeper with those questions and/or even improve what you offer.

How to Bring in Clients and/or Customers

Add Value Consistently

This will build trust and credibility and create a following for what you have to offer, what you have learned, and what you teach. This will create momentum. A good book about this is *The Slight Edge* by Jeff Olson.

You'll also learn so much and gain confidence through teaching and the value you provide.

Show Up Online

People are online all the time. There are billions of people at your fingertips; you must use the internet and social media. You don't have to use every single thing out there, but choose at least two platforms to use. You can use the same content on each and even reuse content. Don't overthink, and don't overcomplicate things for yourself.

Be You and Share Your Story

No matter what you are selling, your story is what will attract people to you. Let's be real here, there are others out there doing what you do and selling what you sell, and there are plenty of customers and clients for everyone. But how will you gain them? Sharing YOU and your story.

This includes your struggles, which can be one of the scariest things you will ever do. We've been taught to stay quiet and only share the highlight reel. That's BS, and it's fake, and what did I say a bunch of times already? Authenticity will win!

"Your struggle is your success!"
– Brendon Buchard

Your story and your struggles are what people will relate to, so share them, but make sure to share how you have overcome them and/or the lessons from them. This doesn't have to be anything extreme. It's the day to day stuff that goes on. It's sharing the reality of trying, failing, learning, and growing.

Show the behind the scenes of the family photo shoot along with the perfectly posed shots.

Stop Comparing

"Comparison is the thief of joy."
– Theodore Roosevelt

You are unique. You have it in you.

Throughout the book, I've asked you some important questions to get you thinking about who you are and what you want. Remember those things, especially when you start looking around at what everyone else is doing, which is very easy to do with social media.

I'm all for looking to others for inspiration, but if you ever start to feel some yucky feelings arise, listen to it, step back, breathe, and think back to who you are, what you want, and take action based on that.

Remember that everyone is on their own path and everyone has their own desires, strengths, and struggles.

Be the Light

There is so much negativity and yuckiness out there. Show up and be the person that others get excited to see because of your positivity and empowerment. I do not mean that everything is rainbows and unicorns, but showing how you work through the crappy times instead of only complaining about them is huge. People need this!

Always think of the energy you are putting out into the world. Do people get the warm and fuzzies? Do they feel inspired and empowered? This is what being the light does, and the world needs more light!

I love this quote by Jesse Elder that sums this up perfectly! "Are you a tugboat? Spending all your time and energy going out to find people and opportunities you want, then trying to haul them back to shore? Or are you a lighthouse… shining so radiantly with your authenticity, power, and clarity that you attract everyone and everything you need to live your purpose? The choice is yours."

You Deserve to Get Paid

Money is not bad. Money is not evil.

Money will not make you happy (you make you happy), but money does give you more opportunity and possibility.

One of the greatest things I had to work on, that I had no idea was a thing, was my money mindset. I had such a messed up view of money from my experiences growing up that I realized I was actually afraid of it. I was afraid people would think all I cared about was money, that I didn't deserve it, that I was materialistic. I thought I would lose friends or that I would get used for my money.

So I stayed broke, and I was afraid to get paid for my services.

Then I began doing the work. I began viewing money as something really good, and more, I began to see what I offered as something worth getting paid for, no matter what anyone else thought. Yes, I encountered people who told me I was a monster for charging for what I did. At first it felt like a punch in the gut, that is until I realized that was all their own money issues, limitations, and false perceptions of me.

And here's what I noticed when people invested versus got stuff for free: They actually did something because they placed a greater value on whatever it is. This usually happens subconsciously, but it happens. When I do free challenges or there's a free webinar, I rarely actually do the work, but when I invest a good amount, you better believe I was listening, taking notes, and taking action.

Because money is a transfer of energy.

I love what one of my business coaches Sara Dann said when I interviewed her on my podcast episode, *Being A Woman That Refuses To Settle*. She said, "It is okay to want more money. It is okay to want to make your own money and to buy the things that you want to… It's okay to want to build and create and live the life that you actually wanted when you were a little girl."

If guilt or yucky feelings around money is something that is coming up for you, get clear on why that is and then recognize how deserving you are of receiving it and all the *good* you can do with it.

"Having a business has shown me I can be more than a mom and show my kids this, which will allow them to be more too. It has opened my mind to see that money can be made in many ways and you don't have to leave your kids or go with what society says is 'right.' I am working from home and making more than what I did as a full time teaching assistant, leaving my kids every day."

– **Shannon Piazza**, mom of 2,
Owner of Mama Finding Her Magic,
mamafindinghermagic.com

Chapter 9

Overcoming Challenges

▪▪▪▪▪

There have been so many times I've wanted to say, "F it!"

Limiting beliefs, negative thoughts, fear, different seasons in my life, barely any likes on my social media content. "Is anybody out there???"

In this chapter, I'm going to share what has kept me going for years, even through all the ups and downs, even when I've felt like I've lost all hope. These are the things that will help you not only rock your biz, but also – your life!

This is the chapter that you'll want to refer to when all the feelings creep in, when people say weird and sometimes crappy things to you, when you feel like you don't have any support, when the haters arise, when all the things start going wrong, and you feel everything is falling apart. Because not all parts of having your own business is sexy, it's important for you to learn how to overcome obstacles and move forward.

My first tip: Do not allow the fact that challenges and struggles will come up, scare you. Let it empower you because it's getting through the struggle that makes you the strong woman you are, and the even stronger one you will become.

You Are Number One

There's been this completely inaccurate belief passed down that we mothers should be putting our kids first or our husbands or the dog. For mothers, all I have seen come from that belief is stress, overwhelm, anxiety, even depression. And I cannot believe this is not talked about more, so I am deciding to.

Your physical and mental health must take priority. Say that to yourself: My physical and mental health must take priority.

This mantra will not only help your business be a success, but your relationships with your kids, your partner, yourself, and others will be better. Plus, every single person you come in contact will be affected positively.

So take care of YOU. Invest in your physical and mental health.

Fuel Your Body with Healthy Whole Foods

There's so much info and a bazillion different diets (I know because I did them all), but it comes down to one thing: Eat real food. What do I mean by that? The majority (and I mean legit majority) needs to be whole foods, not that weird processed stuff where you look on the back of a box and there are 163643681903 ingredients produced in a lab. When you eat that stuff, your body will come back with a big "F you!" in the form of fatigue, bad skin, disease, weight gain, lack of creativity, anxiety, and more. No bueno, girlfriend.

Am I saying eat kale all day every day? No but get real with yourself. The vast majority needs to be real, healthy food, with a lot of veggies and especially greens. This is why I love green smoothies. I can pack them full of goodness every day.

You can also track what and how much you eat (because you need to eat enough). Track how you feel with what you are eating – physically and mentally. You should feel energized, empowered, confident, and happy.

Drink Lots of Water

The rule is at least half your body weight in ounces. For example, if you weigh 135 lbs, then at least about 68 ounces per day. I have a big water bottle I fill and drink from consistently and bring with me everywhere. I don't get all fancy. I just do it.

Move Your Body Daily in Some Way

Cardio, weights, yoga, Pilates, dance, kickbox, whatever… But move your body. Besides the physical health benefits, it'll help your mental state and creativity.

Meditate

If what comes to mind is sitting in complete silence with your legs crossed on the floor and that freaks you out, know that it does not have to be that way. That's what I thought, and it held me back from doing this. You know how you have a bazillion thoughts running through your mind All The Time? Meditation helps you calm that down. It helps you learn how to actually listen to yourself, breathe, and will help get ideas flowing. I needed it so badly, so I began googling, and I found guided meditations that help me. I'm far from perfect with this. Thoughts creep in, but it's learning how to recognize them, that has been the most powerful for me, and there are so many resources out there – YouTube, apps, and more, so take a moment to look for some.

Fuel Your Mind with Empowerment and Positivity Consistently:

- No, you do not need to watch the news, especially not to start your day. I never watch the news. One day I was over my in-laws and the news was on. One minute in and I could feel my vibe dropping significantly.
- What is coming up on your social media feed? You are allowed to unfollow the negativity! Start following the light bringers! And remember to be one yourself as I said in the last chapter.

- Read and listen to empowering books, podcasts, videos, etc.

Get rid of as much negativity as you can, and learn how to block the rest. Think back to being Wonder Woman!

Take time for you. Yes! You can, and you need to.

Please make note of this: The most successful people take really good care of their bodies because if your body is not feeling it's best, there's only so far you will go with anything else. Your body is a temple. Think of what it does and has done for you, and treat her the way she deserves to be treated.

Be Proud

Yeah, that's right! Another BS belief that has been passed down is that you're "full of yourself" or a "narcissist" or whatever else if you feel good about your accomplishments or share them.

You are not. You are allowed to feel so proud of yourself and share that with the world because others need to know what is possible.

This is one of the things that held me back from shining. I was so afraid others would think I was full of myself, so I shrunk – in school, in my business, in my social media posts, everywhere.

Create a Why I'm Awesome (or whatever you'd like to call it) list. I first learned this from one of my coaches Jenn Scalia as a way to build confidence: a reminder of all I had accomplished to show myself how capable I am.

When you feel your confidence slipping or when you start dwelling on mistakes or thinking you can't, pull this list out, and remind yourself how awesome you are.

Add skills, accomplishments, traits, anything. Do not overthink or judge. Let it flow.

I used to think in order to be truly accomplished, I had to cure cancer or something. Nope.

Go all out, have fun, and when you are done, read it and let it sink in. Then put in in a place you will have easy access to in those times I mentioned.

Something I do every day and have my Level Up Ladies (health group clients) do daily is celebrate at least one win (big or small) every day. It's important that we become aware of our daily wins and own our awesomeness. If you do this, you will begin to see all you are capable of.

Beliefs: Yours and Theirs

The reason I've mentioned beliefs so often is because what we believe can either push us forward or keep us stuck. This is going to be an incredibly important part of how you do things, so please make sure to take action on this.

First: Start becoming aware of your beliefs in regards to yourself and your capabilities and what is possible in general. It's easy to catch beliefs that are holding you back because they often start with, "I can't" or "I'm never going to have" or "That could never" or "It's too hard to" or "It's easy for her" or "I'm not good enough to" or "There isn't enough money, time, etc." These are all beliefs you are carrying around and stories you tell yourself that will keep you stuck and hold you back from living the life you deserve.

Also, what stories are you telling yourself? We are really good story maker-uppers, and if you don't realize it, it can hold you back and even ruin relationships.

Have you ever texted someone and didn't hear back, so you immediately go into "OMG she must hate me. What did I do?" mode? And you sit in that story for hours or days?

How about something like this:

One time I was heading out with some friends, and I put on what I believed to be a very cute outfit and asked my husband what he thought. It wasn't the over the top, you look amazing comment I was hoping for, and I immediately thought, "He thinks I look horrible."

A few weeks later when we were going on a date night, he told me to wear that outfit because I looked so hot in it. He wanted me to save the outfit for our date night.

Ahhhhh the stories we tell ourselves. I could write a book about all of mine.

Second: Get really good at recognizing other people's beliefs and how they limit themselves. Do not allow others' stories and limitations to limit you.

Some that really affected me in the past are:

- You can't have kids and a healthy, strong, toned body
- Your life will basically end when you have kids. You won't have a social life, or be able to go anywhere
- You can't stay home with your kids and have your own money
- You can't have money and be happy
- You can't have a thriving business and have time for your family
- You can't eat healthy and be healthy and have a life
- Success = hustle and no freedom

I saw others saying these things, and I started believing them because I allowed their stories and beliefs to get in my head until I said, "Screw that, I'm going to show what's possible." I have, and you can too.

Fear

I interviewed a bunch of mamas for this book. One of the questions I asked was, "What is holding you back from starting a business?" The majority of the answers revolved around the "F" word – fear.

Fear of:

- failing
- the work
- taking time away from family
- asking for financial help from others
- lack of skills
- what others will think
- not being good enough
- success
- losing people
- wasting time
- not knowing what will happen

After reading these, how do you feel? Like you're not alone, right? Of course. Because you are human, and fear is something we feel as humans. These are all possibilities of what could happen when you take the leap.

My biggest tip on this is learning to have faith. Faith will win over fear all day, every day. It took me a while to get it. I honestly didn't even know what faith truly meant until I began making big decisions when it came to my business, and now faith is what gets me through the fear and the self-doubt that comes up a lot.

Also, start turning that fear into excitement for what is possible. Even when everything feels like it's crumbling, as may happen at times, your faith and belief is what will keep you moving forward.

The only way to really overcome fear and gain confidence is to take action. So get to it, girlfriend. And know that other people's opinions and judgments do not matter. Their perceptions of you are just that, their perceptions, which have to do with their beliefs, fears, and insecurities. You will find your people, the ones that love you and support you for being you and what you do. They are the ones that matter!

What are some times you can remember where you worked through your fear? How did you feel after? What did it do for you?

Flip It

Those beliefs, stories, and fears that are holding you back will not hold you back for long when you decide to get really good at flipping them.

When the limiting beliefs, fear, and self-doubt start coming up, you must first be aware of them, then ask yourself some of these questions:

- What are my disempowering beliefs?
- Where is this belief coming from? Is it something I was brought up believing? Was it said to me? Is it something I

hear others say? If it's something others are saying, make sure to consider the source. How's their life going?

- What am I really afraid of? You may need to ask this a few times to get to the core of it, similar to getting to that deep why.
- What are these disempowering beliefs costing me?
- Now your next step is to flip the story, belief, and/or fear into an empowering belief! So now ask yourself these questions:
- What are my new empowering beliefs?
- What beliefs do I need now to take my health, business, life, etc. to the next level?
- How do I know this?
- Some of my empowering beliefs are:
- I can achieve anything and everything. I'm capable and it all comes easy to me. I know this because I know it's all in me, and I have belief and faith.
- I know what to do to [insert goal], and I do it. I know this because I have the tools and help to achieve the goal, and if I don't, I will seek it. I am an action taker.
- I add massive value through my story and inspiration. I create incredible value for clients and followers.
- I'm an amazing leader. I know this because I step up and say what I know needs to be said, and I lead by example.

- I can handle all that is thrown at me. I know this because I have overcome a lot, and I am strong.

The idea of writing a book had been on my mind for a few years, but I kept saying things like, "I'm not a writer," "What if I get bad reviews?," "It won't be as good as [insert authors], so what's the point?," "It's a big investment, and what if I don't make any money?," and on and on and on. Then I had a moment when my faith and belief and my passion for my message and movement became stronger. That's when I flipped my thoughts to, "I need to get this out there for me and for the many women that will benefit from it. I'm amazing and my message is important. Those that need it will love it. The others don't matter."

Be the Woo Girl

I'm not talking about when you're out and your fave songs comes on, although I do hope that this is happening for you still. I'm talking about believing in something greater than you.

This idea was something I was so closed off to. I refused to open my eyes and see that I really had so much help. But more, I saw how powerful I could be if I would just open myself up to it all.

I notice signs a lot. Signs that I'm where I need to be and on the right track and signs that show me the universe has my back (Note: *The Universe Has Your Back* is an amazing book by Gabrielle Bernstein).

I don't remember why, but this year I chose orchids as a sign for me. Whenever I saw them, it was a reminder that I was indeed on the right path and that I should continue to trust myself. I was preparing for a trip to a Tony Robbins event, and I kept questioning myself. "Should I really go? I could use the money for something else. I don't want to leave my kids." And on and on.

My husband and kids drop me off at the airport, I step up to get my boarding pass only to see that my flight is cancelled. There is no other flight that day, but I could fly into another airport two and a half hours away from the event.

I could have taken that as a sign to not go, but instead, I figured it out. I booked that other flight, had my husband pick me back up, went and got food, and rented a car (a convertible because I was going to Florida, so why would I not). The flight was smooth, the drive was nice, and when I arrived at the hotel, orchids were the first thing I saw. Boom! And that event changed my life. It was there that I decided to have another baby and write this book. I'm currently 20 weeks pregnant with my third child as I write this story.

Life becomes so much more fun and fulfilling when you live it this way.

TATI TIP! **When you decide to step up and take your life to another level, your brain likes to come up with reasons why not to keep you safe and comfy. Know that, and step up anyway.**

Law of Attraction

"Where Focus Goes, Energy Flows."
– Tony Robbins

(That man knows his stuff. I could listen to him talk for hours, and I have, ha ha.)

* * *

What are you focusing on? The negatives? The challenges? Do you find yourself saying things like, "When it rains, it pours?"

All these questions do is bring in more negativity and challenges. I'm not saying challenges won't arise, but a great way to cope with them is acknowledging them and seeing them as a learning experience and something to overcome versus throwing yourself into victim mode.

One of my favorite questions to ask myself is, "Why is this happening for me?" Not to me but for me. By asking myself that question, I will create a learning experience versus a pity party. You'll also begin to notice how more of the good stuff will start coming your way instead! Yay! Because what you put out, you get back. It's a law, the law of attraction. So think of what you want to attract into your life. Then put those thoughts out there. Believe in all that is possible for you, and watch the magic begin to happen.

This is one the greatest lessons I have learned, so check yourself. What vibes are you putting out there, and what are you getting back in return?

Who Are You Hangin With?

I went out to eat with my girl a couple weeks ago. The waitress came over at least three times before we actually ordered. Each time she did, we'd look at each other and say, "Um… We haven't even looked at the menu." That's how into our convo we were. This always happens with her, and the other women I hang with. We get so deep and passionate that we usually end up closing the place. Note: These convos are about what we are going through – the good and the bad, to listen and hold space and give advice (and even get challenged) when needed, vulnerability, love, and some booty-kicking when needed.

I cannot stress how important it is to be aware of who you surround yourself with because they are you. Want to be healthy and fit? Do your friends place value on their health and take care of themselves? Or are they constantly falling off the wagon or pushing crappy food on you and saying it's okay to skip the workout?

Take an inventory of the people you're surrounding yourself. Are they living the lives, doing the things, and acting the way you want to be?

Are you hanging with people that enable you? Do they call you out on how you're holding yourself back (and are you allowing them to do this) because they want to see you kill it in life and be truly happy?

Note: It's okay to let people go. It's okay to distance yourself. What's not okay is sticking around people that are toxic because you think you have to and this includes family members. Again, it is okay to shed people from your life that are not bringing in the vibes you desire for your life.

I have a rule that I only hang out with high vibe, woke AF, empowered, authentic, confident women that are working on themselves – body and mind – consistently and push me to be better. This does not mean they are perfect and their lives are perfect, but they don't hang out in Victimville or play the blame game or create drama or talk bad about others all day long. They work through the challenges, learn, and grow, and we do it together.

By the way, that is not the easiest. I have felt guilt. I have felt like a I was being mean. I have questioned myself. But in the end, I know who I want to be, how I want my life to be, and I understand the importance of who I hang with.

So remember that you are not mean or selfish for saying, "Bye bye." You are up-leveling yourself and your life.

Your Identity

I used to envision myself as a sexy, confident, woman who lived life on her terms, but I allowed all the stuff like self-doubt and fear get in the way. So my identity for a very long time was basically me speaking really mean myself.

That is until I began doing the work on myself and specifically envisioning the woman I would become and how she would act. I began acting like a sexy, confident, woman who lives life on her terms. This is the woman who:

- Takes care of her body. She eats well and exercises consistently.
- Fuels her mind with empowering information and is consistently learning
- Says what she wants and go after what she wants
- Hangs with other women who are up leveling their lives
- Sets boundaries and isn't a people-pleaser
- Asks for help
- Looks for solutions

- Is not afraid of failing and takes on challenges
- Knows she is capable of anything she sets her mind to
- Speaks her mind
- Is open minded
- Is a leader
- Is abundant and grateful
- Is truly happy
- Owns who she is

I want you to think about your identity, which is basically how you describe yourself. It's what you believe about yourself and your capabilities. If what you come up with isn't something that makes you feel freaking amazing, then you need to create a new one.

Write out that identity, and then list the traits of that identity. Then start acting like her now.

Decide

There's a huge difference between saying you want something or will do something and making a decision. It's not "I'll try until it gets hard or scary." When you decide to do something, it's happening no matter what. This doesn't mean that it will necessarily happen in a way you think or want it to, but you know it will, and you will do everything to make it happen.

TATI TIP! **Release expectation. Instead surrender, and again, have faith, belief, and trust in yourself and the universe.**

Everything Is Figureoutable

Marie Forleo, an amazing entrepreneur, said that. It stuck with me ever since I heard it and is something I say every single time a challenge come up.

I no longer throw in the towel. I figure it out instead. Because when you've made a decision, this is what you do.

Examples:

- No money to start or get the help I need → How do I get it?
- No support or the kinds of people I need around me → Where do I find them?
- I have too much on my plate → Who can I ask for help?
- It's overwhelming → What steps can I begin to take now?
- That didn't work → What can I do instead? What can I do next?
- No time → What can I do to create more time? What do I need to say, "No" to? What can I ask for help with? Where do I need to set boundaries?
- I don't know what to do → What do I need to do to figure this out?

- I'm stuck → What's keeping me stuck? Fear? Limiting beliefs? My stories?
- I don't know what to do → Where can you find help? Who can you get help from?

As my girl, Kelly Joseph says, "Become solution savvy. There is a solution for everything."

There will be challenges that come up. That's exactly why I want to arm you with all of this to help you take action and move forward. Just remember your vision and your why and have a burning desire for what you do.

You now have the knowledge and tools to move forward, and you are powerful. Own that. Your next step? Go for it!

"My mind is the single most debilitating obstacle if you let it be – or the greatest tool you have if you build it up. So I chose to build it up. But to this day, I still have the voice in my head that questions me – until I kick it out and flip it! I used to fear more what others though – used to think I was unworthy of the level of success that I truly desired – and that it was not about the money – or the things – until recently in the past year – I really dove into my mindset. I hired coaches. Took courses. Went to events. And decided I had to do better for myself – and really level up. My business has given me time freedom, more family time, a healthier marriage – actually super passionate relationship with my man because I decided to show up for me – to follow my passion in life, and so he started showing up completely different for me too. Now we are better than ever. I'm lit up in life and love and as a mom and a human in general."

– **Erin Call**, mom of 3,
Owner of of Erin Call Coaching – Spiritual CEO,
erincallcoaching.com

Conclusion

You Can Do This!

■■■■■

My mother left Cuba in the 1960's when it became a dictatorship and everything (ever-y-thing) was taken from her and her family. Her parents had been allowed into the United States as refugees, but she had to go to another country first. So she left Cuba and went to Spain with only a few pieces of clothing. While there, she went door to door selling Gillette razors to make money. She would come home with blisters from walking in shoes that were losing their soles, yet she continued to do it. Less than a year later she was able to come to the United States, where she worked at my grandparents' clothing factory. Deciding she wanted more, she applied to the local community college, but due to her lack of knowledge of English, they told her she could not. Not taking no for an answer, she kept going for it and made it happen. Not only did she go to the community college, but she ended up getting a PHD in nuclear engineering and was pregnant with me in graduate school. She later became a single mother, worked full time, and dealt with a lot being a Hispanic woman in a white male-dominated field. Then in her 60's, she discovered her passion for cooking, wrote a cookbook, and at 72, decided to get her cooking out into the world by buying a bakery. My mom never gave up. Ever. And I grew up not only hearing her tell me the importance of that but seeing her do it!

I learned some big lessons from her story: 1. Your circumstances do not dictate your life. You do. 2. If you truly want something, you'll find a way. 3. Show up, even when it's tough. 4. It's never too late to start new things and grow, but you do have to want to, and you must take action. 5. You don't have to be like everyone else, and that is where your magic is.

You have learned a lot throughout this book. You've learned how to get clarity on what it is you want for yourself and a business, who you will help, why, and how! You've recognized obstacles that may come up and how to deal with them. You've also realized that getting your service or product in front of your ideal client is a gift for them and how to feel good doing it! A business is only truly successful when you feel good about it!

It's time, mama. Don't wait. Now is the time to take action. You have a feeling inside you. Listen to it. Go for it. Or you'll wake up one day wishing you had.

Whatever it is that you decide you want for your business, your life, and your family's life, is possible. You have it in you to make anything happen. Become that woman you know is inside of you waiting to show herself and the world what she is capable of!

You are allowed to want more. You are allowed to change. You are allowed to step up.

Do not allow yourself, or anyone else, to hold you back.

And whatever you do – do not give up! The world needs your magic. The world needs the light you will bring to it by going after your dreams, being unapologetically yourself, and truly happy!

You don't have to have it all together.

Believe. Trust. Have Faith. Take massive, imperfect action, and watch it all unfold.

Now go out and contribute! To your family, to the world, and most importantly, to yourself!

When you do, you are going to learn so much about yourself. You are going to grow, and you will become truly happy.

You deserve it all.

"I built my business as a stay at home mom, and although it was full of challenges, I woke up every day excited to work on my business. Besides it becoming what supports our family financially, my business has truly changed every area of our life, and has brought me passion and purpose. I love being a mom, but I know how important it is for me to pursue my unique passions in life. I want my kids to grow up knowing that their mom worked hard to create a life that fills her up each and every day. I want them to see that you can be a good mom, and a successful business owner. It doesn't have to be one or the other."

– **Lindsey Robinson**, mom of 3,
Owner of of Lindsey Robinson Photography
at lindseyrobinsonphotography.com

Acknowledgments

There have been so many influential and supportive people in my life who have helped me in recognizing what I'm capable of and get things done!

Thank you to my mom, Rosa! You have shown me that our circumstances do not dictate our lives and that it is important to go against the norm, do what you love at any age, and rise up in the face of any challenge! Thank you for being different from all the other moms when I was growing up. I didn't realize it back then, but it showed me that I don't have to be like everyone else, and I can be a mom and do more. Thank you for always supporting me and telling me how capable I am!

To my incredible husband, Christian. No matter what I say I want to do, you have supported me. You have never once questioned my dreams and decisions and have helped me make it all happen by being the amazing father and husband you are!

To my kids. I want to make this world a better place for you, for your kids, grandchildren, and on and on. Because of you, I decided that I need to be truly happy, and you are the reason I decided to take care of myself – body and mind – and go after my dreams and desires. I want to show you that you must take care of yourselves, do whatever it is you want to do in your lives, and that you are deserving and capable of all of it! You are amazing!

To my in-laws and sister-in-law. Thank you for loving on my kids like you do and for all of the help you have given. It's easy to ask for help when I know I have people in my life that love to give it!

To my Level Up Ladies and all my clients. Thank you for deciding to make yourselves a priority, and thank you for entrusting in me to help you believe in yourselves and call you out on how you're holding yourselves back when you needed me to. Thank you for listening, and thank you for taking action. It is incredible to watch you grow!

To my team, Have It All Tribe, especially to those of you that have been with me through all the ups and downs, stuck around, and continue to show up! You are making the world a better place by deciding to work on yourselves and help others work on themselves. The ripple effect we are creating is pretty awesome, and I'm excited for all that is to come!

To my girl, Kelly Joseph. Thank you for asking me to meet you at the park that one day with our boys. I can't imagine doing any of this without you and your light. You are an amazing, strong, determined woman that refuses to allow anything get in her way, and I love watching you grow! You have been with me from the beginning, and it's been pretty amazing knowing all we have been through and that we are still here going strong, even through all the challenges! I'm so excited for what the universe has in store for us!

To my ladies, Ashley, Kat, and Shannon. Thank you for the daily reminder that women can be cool, supportive of each other, and drama free! Having a solid group of women that love on each other and help each other out pretty much daily is the best!

To all my coaches and mentors – Jenn Scalia, Sara Dann, Amanda Daley, and the many more. Thank you for helping me see my BS and stop holding myself back. You are all incredible women showing other entrepreneurs what is possible! I would not have gotten to where I have gotten without your guidance and push!

To Angela Lauria and the Author Incubator team. Thank you for creating an epic program that has helped me create this book – something I have been wanting to do for so long and clearly needed the universe to put you in front of me to make it happen the way it needed to! Thank you for all of your guidance and support.

To the Morgan James Publishing team: Special thanks to David Hancock, CEO & Founder for believing in me and my message. To my Author Relations Manager, Tiffany Gibson, thanks for making the process seamless and easy. Many more thanks to everyone else, but especially Jim Howard, Bethany Marshall, and Nickcole Watkins.

Thank you to all the amazing female entrepreneurs I follow that show up, don't allow anyone to knock you down, inspire me, and have shown me what is possible! Thank you for being transparent in what building a business looks like and for showing the world what we women are capable of!

Thank you to everyone in my communities and all over social media that have given me love and supported me, especially when sharing my most vulnerable moments!

Thank you, my reader for picking up this book, and more – for opening up your mind, deciding that you want more in your life! You are brave, you are strong, and you are capable of having all it is you want in and for your life!

Thank You!

Thanks so much for reading. The fact that you've gotten to this point in the book tells me something important about you: You're ready. You're ready to start making some changes in your life and stepping up into a new level by building a business!

It's now time for you to put everything you've read into action, and I have some additional resources to help you do that over at **tatianaamico.com/book**.

When you head over there, you get access to:

- Workbooks, videos, and more
- Access to my free Facebook community for women like you that want to truly live their lives. As I said in the book, surrounding yourself with like-minded women is incredibly important.
- Gain access to my VIP email list to ensure you see all the goods I'm putting out, including exclusive workshops, videos, events, and so much more
- Discover how you can continue to learn and grow, and how you can get my help to build a successful business you love

I'm so excited for you!

xo,

Tatiana

About the Author

Tatiana Amico is a mother who understands firsthand what life as a busy mom is like, who also has desires for more, who is passionate about showing other mothers what is possible for them, and that they can create the lives they desire. She decided to leave corporate America and become a stay-at-home mom with her first son. Soon after, she realized she was meant to do more and wanted to help her family financially. So, she decided to start a business from home to contribute financially while still being able to care for her son.

She is a certified health coach, successful entrepreneur, influencer, speaker, podcaster, and business mentor. She specializes in helping women gain clarity on what it is they want in their lives, see their potential, take action, and see massive results.

Tatiana has been trained and mentored by some of the most incredible coaches in the world. She believes that creating a better world begins with individuals taking care of themselves – body and mind. In 2014, she joined a health and fitness network marketing company. She built up a highly successful business quickly by helping hundreds of women with their health and building a team of wellness entrepreneurs.

Tatiana believes every woman is deserving and capable of going after more and living a life they desire and deserve. She is excited to now take all of her skills and help women step up in their lives, go after their dreams, and make money building businesses they love!

Here's how you can contact Tatiana Amico:
Website: tatianaamico.com
Email: tatiana.amico@gmail.com
Facebook: fb.com/Tatiana.amico.5
Instagram: instagram.com/tatianaamico